Latin and Ballroom

Susie Hodge

Heinemann

www.heinemannlibrary.co.uk
Visit our website to find out more information about **Heinemann Library** books.

To order:
☎ Phone 44 (0) 1865 888066
🖹 Send a fax to 44 (0) 1865 314091
🖥 Visit the Heinemann Bookshop at www.heinemannlibrary.co.uk to browse our catalogue and order online.

Heinemann Library is an imprint of Capstone Global Library Limited, a company incorporated in England and Wales having its registered office at 7 Pilgrim Street, London, EC4V 6LB – Registered company number: 6695582

Heinemann is a registered trademark of Pearson Education Limited, under licence to Capstone Global Library Limited

Text © Capstone Global Library Limited 2008
First published in hardback in 2008
Paperback edition first published in 2010

Editorial: Sarah Shannon and Robyn Hardyman
Design: Steve Mead and Geoff Ward
Picture Research: Maria Joannou
Production: Duncan Gilbert

Originated by Modern Age Repro House Ltd
Printed and bound by Leo Paper Products Ltd

ISBN 978 0431 933 115 (Hardback)
12 11 10 09 08
10 9 8 7 6 5 4 3 2 1

ISBN 978 0431 933 191 (Paperback)
14 13 12 11 10
10 9 8 7 6 5 4 3 2 1

British Library Cataloguing in Publication Data
Hodge, Susie,
Latin and ballroom. - (Dance)
793.3'3

A full catalogue record for this book is available from the British Library.

Acknowledgements
The publishers would like to thank the following for permission to reproduce photographs: © Alamy Images pp.**32** (Sami Sarkis Travel America), **34** (Visual Arts Library London), **37** (kolvenbach), **38** (Geoff A Howard); © Art Archive p. **7** (Musée des Beaux Arts Troyes/Gianni Dagli Orti); © Bridgeman Art Library p. **10** (Private Collection, Index); © Corbis pp. **4** (Dimitri Iundt/TempSport), **5** (Robbie Jack), **14** (Burstein Collection), **15**, **17** (Bettmann), **23** (Underwood & Underwood), **27**, **30** (epa/Eddy Risch), **41** (Jason Redmond/Reuters), **45** (Luis Enrique Ascui/Reuters); © Getty Images pp. **18** (Firmin/Topical Press Agency), **21** (Gjon Mili/Time Life Pictures), **26** (AFP Photo/Juan Mabromata) , **36** (AFP Photo/Vanderlei Almeida); © Lebrecht Music & Arts Photolibrary p. **25** (Ilian Iliev); © Mary Evans Picture Library pp. **8**, **12** (Steve Rumney); © Reuters pp. **22**, **28** (Chaiwat Subprasom), **43** (Luis Enrique Ascui); © Rex Features pp. **19** (Everett Collection), **29**; © Still Pictures p. **40** (VISUM/Gustavo Alabiso); © Topham Picturepoint p. **16**.

Cover photograph of dancers at the samba show 'Brasil Brasileiro' in 2006, reproduced with permission of © Photoshot/Starstock.

Every effort has been made to contact copyright holders of any material reproduced in this book. Any omissions will be rectified in subsequent printings if notice is given to the publishers.

Contents

Some words are printed in bold, **like this**. You can find out what they mean by looking in the glossary, on page 46.

A dance for everyone

Dancing is one of the most beautiful and uplifting art forms. The right mix of music, **rhythm** and movement can be stunning. Primitive tribes used rhythm to express emotion and tell stories, and gradually **folk** and peasant dances spread through more developed societies. Dance became less of a ritual and more of a way to celebrate and socialize.

Stage and screen

Ballroom dancing is a set of dances where two people, usually a man and a woman, partner each other. Latin dance emerged as part of this, and now both Latin and ballroom performances are watched on stage, in film and on television by millions of viewers around the world. The appeal of Latin and ballroom dance has grown, and one of its greatest attractions is that everyone can enjoy it. It holds no barriers to age or language. Classes, competitions and shows have increased its appeal – but what makes it so compelling? Every popular dance originates from a great rhythm and, as far as it can be traced, every successful ballroom dance has been adapted from a folk dance. Initially these folk dances came from Europe. Over time they developed into more formal dances, eventually appearing in ballrooms.

◄ A couple dancing the Viennese waltz – traditionally, they rotate around the ballroom. New waltz steps include side-swaying and underarm turns.

Regulating dances

Ballroom and Latin dancing is one of the most popular pastimes in the world. Since dance competitions first appeared in around 1907, they have become widespread. The Imperial Society of Dance Teachers (as it was first known) was formed in July 1904 in London. In 1924, the ballroom branch was created to standardize the music, steps and techniques of the dances. There are now ten dances classed as 'International Standard' and 'International Latin', which are the official, approved terms worldwide. In 1988 the term 'DanceSport' came into use to describe competitive ballroom and Latin American dancing (see pages 42–3).

Ballroom and Latin dancing is influenced by events, such as changes in fashion, music and society, and by the popularity of films or television programmes. New dances either spread and grow – or they disappear. Some develop from unstructured, casual dances, while others are adopted and adapted 'on the street' from ballrooms. As they catch on, they eventually become recognized dances. Across the world, there are two variations that are recognized styles of Latin and ballroom dance: the 'American Smooth' and 'American Rhythm'. The steps and movements in these dances have been **regulated** into internationally agreed techniques, rhythms and **tempos**.

▲ The Argentine Tango is a social dance that first developed in the city of Buenos Aires. The steps are expressive and spirited.

Dance Facts

Main dances

The main ballroom dances are the waltz, tango, Viennese waltz, foxtrot, quick-step, cha-cha-cha, polka and schottische.

The main Latin dances are samba, rumba, paso doble, jive, East Coast swing, bolero, mambo and salsa.

First steps

Social or group dancing has probably existed in some form since the beginning of human society. Two sorts of dance evolved as cultures developed: celebration or ceremonial dances and magical or religious dances. The medicine men of primitive cultures, such as the Native Americans, who danced to call for their god's assistance, were possibly the first **choreographers**. As society and human conditions change, so do communal dances. Contemporary social dancing reflects life now just as much as primitive dancing reflected life hundreds of years ago.

Early social dancing

Early in history, **folk dancing** was for the lower classes, while social dancing was for the privileged. But during the 14th century, popular folk dances of the lower classes moved into upper-class homes in England as part of evening entertainment. People danced in rings around the central hearth. When chimneys became more widespread in the 14th century, the hearth moved against a side wall, clearing the floor and allowing **processional dances**, where people marched and danced in lines following each other.

Throughout Europe in the 15th and 16th centuries, during social dances, couples started dancing close to each other. The 'basse' dance of the 15th century was probably the first recognized dance to do this. It was a deliberate and dignified dance for the **aristocracy** to show off their breeding and splendour. When performing the basse dance, couples moved quietly and gracefully in a slow gliding or walking motion, raising and lowering their bodies. It originated in the Italian courts and soon spread throughout Europe.

Royal steps

'Official' dances first began in the royal courts. Anyone who wanted to dance at court studied and copied the latest dances, and the dances soon spread. By the 16th century, dancing had become an essential part of social behaviour. It was particularly associated with royal courts, although the first published book on ballroom dancing was written by a priest! (See page 9.)

(See page 9.)

▼ Dancing in the 16th century could be quite formal in wealthy circles. Everyone knew the steps.

7

15th-century guidance

There aren't many records of actual dances from the 15th century. However, there is one book dating from that century that was written by an Italian knight and dancing master, Domenico da Piacenza. He wrote that the three most important aspects of dancing are measure (understanding the **tempo** of the music), memory (remembering the steps and their order) and manner (matching your manner to the style of the dance).

Two of da Piacenza's students, Antonio Cornazano and Guglielmo Ebreo da Pesaro, wrote more dancing books. Da Pesaro described the female's role: 'Her glance should not be proud or

During the reign of Louis XIV, ballet emerged as a great sensation. Louis himself performed in ballets. Here he is dressed as the Sun. As a result he styled himself 'the Sun King'.

wayward, gazing here or there as many do. Let her, for the most part keep her eyes, with decency, on the ground...' In the 15th century, a woman's place in society was very different from a man's!

The dancing priest

In France in 1588, writing under the pen name 'Thoinot-Arbeau', a Catholic priest called Jehan Tabourot published *Orchesographie*. This book described several of the popular social dances of the time. Some of these replaced the basse dance, including the energetic branle, tourdion and galliarde. Arbeau wrote that certain techniques were made up by dancing masters, but no dance was 'set' rigidly at that time – everyone did their own versions.

It was not until the second half of the 17th century that rigid rules for dances were laid down. The first detailed instruction manual, *The English Dancing Master* by John Playford, appeared in 1651. It contained the music and instructions for 105 English country dances. It helped to popularize these dances, to the extent that they dominated Western ballrooms for the next 150 years. The book made a great difference to the social life of the upper classes in England.

Technique

Ballet and ballroom divide
By the end of the 17th century, Louis XIV of France had founded the Académie Royale de Musique et de Danse (Royal Academy of Music and Dance) and rules were laid down for the first time. Members of the Académie worked out particular steps and techniques. One of the first rules was the five positions of the feet, now used in ballet. From this time, ballet was no longer performed in ballrooms, as **professional** dancers began performing it on stage. Steps, techniques and entire dances divided into ballet or ballroom, although the influence of ballet lasted for over two centuries.

Danse du salon

To a certain extent, dances changed to suit contemporary fashions and fashions changed to suit certain dances. In 17th-century Europe, heels were added to shoes and clothes became less restrictive, affecting the way people walked and danced.

▼ All young ladies and gentlemen learned to dance. In the 18th century, the steps involved occasionally holding a partner's hand and doing simple steps, such as turning or pointing the toes.

Closed hold

Upper-class men wore swords when they were dancing! The sword was worn on the left, so it's possible that the **closed hold** was developed to accommodate it. The closed hold is where the man's left hand holds his partner's right hand high. The woman's left hand rests on the top of the man's right upper arm and his right hand rests on her back. But any hold must have been awkward with the sword clanking about!

Dancing masters

Although ballroom dance steps were not clearly fixed until the 17th century, dancing masters had been teaching dancing for at least 200 years. During the 17th century, dancing masters taught ballet to **professional** dancers and the *danse du salon* (the French term for ballroom dancing) to ladies and gentlemen in their homes, preparing them for balls and parties. Dancing masters advertised in newspapers or were hired when previous pupils recommended them. Although at the time most dances only consisted of about a dozen steps, certain steps and sequences had to be learned. Usually the man performed a sequence of steps which were then repeated by the woman, then the entire dance was repeated, with the woman doing everything first. Most dances were quite similar, although they were modified for different **rhythms** and **tempos**.

In both Europe and America, Italian and French dancing masters were considered the best teachers, as court dancing had started in France and Italy in the 16th century. When French **aristocrats** escaped to America during the French Revolution (with no money, belongings or skills), all they could offer were their dancing skills, so many became dancing masters.

Meeting places

Only the aristocracy went to balls, but by the 1890s assemblies were held in church halls, and in some countries public dance halls began opening for everyone. Soon, people of all classes were twirling around to the music of minuets, quadrilles, polkas and waltzes. Dances and balls were opportunities to socialize, wear new clothes and meet potential husbands and wives.

The minuet

Ballroom dances in the 17th century were planned and formal. The minuet was particularly formal. Men and women danced the minuet hand in hand, following a complex pattern of steps. Louis XIV danced it in public in Paris in 1653, and this set the seal on its respectability. The name came from the French word *menuet*, meaning pretty and delicate, as the dance is made up of small, graceful steps.

▲ The exhilaration of dancing the waltz gradually overcame many of its critics, although the close hold was still considered shocking by some.

The waltz

In the 19th century, the waltz arrived from Vienna and then spread rapidly around Europe. For the first time, couples turned towards each other and away from other dancers, the man intimately holding the waist of his partner. All ballroom dances after the waltz used a similar hold. The gliding, waltzing movements immediately became a craze. Unlike more courtly dances with their controlled steps, the waltz allowed performers to swirl around the dance floor, setting their own boundaries and patterns.

At first, the waltz had many critics. Unlike the minuet and other court dances, which needed considerable practice, the steps could be learned quickly. Dancing masters saw this as a threat. The close hold of the woman by the man shocked some people, and many religious leaders regarded it as sinful. It was even banned in parts of Germany and Switzerland. An article in *The Times* newspaper in England (1816), stated: 'We remarked with pain that the indecent foreign dance called the Waltz was introduced... it is quite sufficient to cast one's eyes on the voluptuous intertwining of the limbs and close compressure on the bodies in the dance... we feel it a duty to warn every parent against exposing his daughter to so fatal a contagion.'

Despite such criticism, the waltz could not be stopped. It has remained the longest-surviving dance.

Wild about waltzing

In the 19th century both the English writers Jane Austen and Lord Byron wrote about the waltz. Queen Victoria had a particular passion for it and thought Prince Albert waltzed beautifully, but it was still considered a shocking dance by many because of its close physical contact. At least one book recommended that unmarried ladies should never do it!

Dance Facts

Waltz origins
Some believe that the waltz originated with the volta, a dance which spread from Italy in the early 16th century. Shakespeare mentions it and it was the favourite dance of both Elizabeth I and Mary, Queen of Scots. Others think that the waltz evolved from an Austro-German dance called the Ländler.

By the 1840s some lively dances from Central Europe, including the polka, mazurka and the schottische, joined the waltz, giving dancers a chance to gallop, swirl and hop across ballrooms. However, all of these dances were tame compared with what was to come.

Strong rhythms

At the end of the 19th century, private balls in the United States featured calm, slow dances that had spread from Europe. Then, in the 1890s, **ragtime** music emerged in African-American communities. Ragtime was a mix of European folk (traditional) music and African drum rhythms. It was refreshing and exhilarating to dance to, and people loved it.

There are several suggestions as to why this style of music was called 'rag' time, but no one really knows the

◄ *The Dance at Bougival* by Auguste Renoir, 1883. In the 19th century, young Parisians met at open-air cafés to dance under the trees.

reason. It may be because the first published piece of ragtime music was called *Mississippi Rag*. It was composed by William H. Krell and published in 1897. The leading composer of the ragtime era was Scott Joplin, who was the son of a slave. In 1902 Joplin wrote *The Entertainer*, which even now is the best-known ragtime number. Unlike the refined music of the minuet or waltz, ragtime was jaunty and exhilarating. It made dancing fun and accessible for both men and women, rich and poor, old and young. Ragtime went on to form the basis of some later Latin dances.

▲ Dancing became more relaxed during the early 20th century. This is Irene and Vernon Castle, dancing in 1914. This American couple spread the new dance crazes, and Irene also led the way in new fashion trends (see page 35).

Famous Dances

Jiggling and wiggling

Elegant European dances had insisted on holding one's body tall and straight. Now, at the beginning of the 20th century, boisterous new dances that mimicked animal movements, such as the Turkey Trot, Grizzly Bear and Chicken Scratch, were the latest thing. These early ragtime dances, with their jiggling and wiggling, were considered improper by many, but were irresistible to even more. Like the music, ragtime dances came from the black communities of America, where many had arrived as slaves. Dance teachers were furious, as the dances did not require hours of expensive lessons. Instead, the simple steps could be learned by watching other dancers, or made up on the spot.

▲ Tea dances remained popular throughout the 20th century. The waltz, rumba and tango were the favourite dances. This tea dance is at the Savoy Hotel, London, in 1912.

Tea dances

From the end of the 19th century, in towns and cities across Europe and the United States, tea dances became all the rage. Private afternoon parties had grown into large ballroom and dance hall gatherings, where people drank tea, ate sandwiches – and danced. Dance trends quickly spread as a result of these events.

Tango teas

One of the first crazes was for a sultry dance called the tango. This dance emerged from Argentina in the 1890s as a dance of seduction. It was a blend of different dances by Argentinian, Italian, Spanish and African immigrants. Proud and passionate, with bodies straight and pressed together and eye contact intense, the tango became a favourite dance in the United States and Europe in the early 20th century. As soon as they saw the exotic steps, everyone wanted to learn how to do it and tango classes sprang up everywhere. The most popular tea dances were soon advertised as 'tango teas' and people flocked to them. With the arrival of World War I in 1914, however, the tango seemed frivolous and came to an abrupt halt – for the time being at least.

Hot and sultry

The tango was just one of many Latin American dances that became popular in the early 20th century. Others included the bolero, lambada, macarena, mambo, merengue and salsa. These dances were fiery and passionate, and many people considered them wicked. Most of the dances had emerged when American immigrants danced their own versions of ancient sacred dances. Over time, each dance's characteristics, such as wriggling and swaying hips, became mixed with the country jigs and clog dances that white settlers brought with them from Europe. When the tango spread to Europe and the United States, it was modified into a form called 'ballroom tango'. This involved less body contact than the Argentinian version, but it still shocked many. In 1922, guidelines were set for the 'English' (international) style of ballroom tango.

▶ Before World War I, the tango was a popular dance. These dancers are in New York.

Dance Facts

Two tango facts

1. In the Argentinian tango, the lady holds her head well back and turned to the side. The reason for this **posture**, originally, was that the gauchos (Argentinian cowboys) smelled so bad it was necessary to turn away from the smell.

2. In 1913, if German army or navy personnel danced the tango, they could be dismissed.

World sensation

The foxtrot is an elegant and graceful dance with a slow-slow-quick-quick-slow **rhythm**. It was invented in 1914, just before the outbreak of World War I, by an American dancer, Harry Fox. He performed in vaudeville (popular shows that consisted of several short acts). He was having difficulty finding a partner for a fast dance, so he incorporated some slow steps. Within a short time, people began dancing their own versions of 'Fox's trot'. The elegant foxtrot soon became all the rage. Men on leave from the War relaxed and socialized while dancing the foxtrot.

Stepping up

In the first few years of its existence, the foxtrot consisted of four slow, strutting steps and then eight quick steps. By 1916 it had developed into a slower, more elegant dance. During the 1920s it took some of the fast jazzy hops and skips of the fashionable charleston and was named the 'quick-time foxtrot and charleston'. Eventually this became the quickstep, which is similar to the foxtrot. The foxtrot and the quickstep were free and light, and suited to the jazz music that was crossing to Europe from America.

▶ These partners have entered a dance competition in the 1920s. They are ready to perform the loose, carefree foxtrot.

The charleston

The charleston is thought to have originated in the Cape Verde Islands near Africa. It had developed into a lively dance performed by African dock workers in the port of Charleston, South Carolina. Men and women danced it freely, changing partners mid-routine. At the end of World War I in 1918, with so many young men dead, many women had to take on men's roles. They worked, cut their hair, wore short skirts and danced the charleston. In Paris in the 1920s, the dancer Josephine Baker popularized the charleston. It spread worldwide, but it was so wild that many ballrooms either banned it or put up signs saying 'PCQ', meaning 'Please Charleston Quietly'!

▲ The charleston is a lively, fun dance that became popular after World War I.

Famous Dances

Quickstep

The quickstep took steps from two other dances as well as the foxtrot. One was the Black Bottom. This dance originated in a place that no longer exists, called Black Bottom, in Detroit and became a sensation after appearing in the stage show *Scandals* in 1926. The other dance was the shimmy, which was probably derived from the Nigerian dance the *Shika*, and taken to America by slaves. The name shimmy is said to have come from a dancer called Gilda Gray who, when asked by a reporter what she shook in the dance, replied, 'My chemise.' A chemise was an undergarment.

Swing

In 1926 the Savoy Ballroom opened in New York. Unlike other dance venues, it welcomed people of all races. Jazz music was new and exciting, and it was an immediate success there. Dancing to jazz was different from any previous dances because men swirled their partners around, lifting and twisting them in a lively way. The style of jazz music that had a strong flow rather than a hard beat became known as swing, and the dance that accompanied it adopted the same name.

Swing music and dances came from both African and European roots – with general features, but no set steps. As swing developed, different versions emerged. So, for example, East Coast swing is a combination of the lindy hop (see below), the foxtrot, the charleston and even the waltz and the tango. The West Coast swing can be danced to almost any kind of music, and is slower than East Coast swing, with steps including taps, shuffles and push-and-pull actions.

Although it lost popularity after 1945, swing has become absorbed into ballroom classifications.

Lindy hop

Lindy hop is an African-American dance that emerged in New York City in the late 1920s. It was based on jazz and the charleston. One evening in 1927, a local dance enthusiast called 'Shorty George' Snowden was watching couples dancing at the Savoy Ballroom. A reporter asked him what dance they were doing. Snowden happened to glance at a nearby newspaper and saw the headline 'Lindy Hops the Atlantic'. It was an article about Charles Lindbergh's recent solo flight from New York to Paris. George simply replied, 'lindy hop'.

In 1934 a spirited version of the dance was named the jitterbug by the band leader Cab Calloway when he introduced a tune called 'Jitterbug'. Contemporary jazz and swing music suited the lindy hop and jitterbug dances perfectly. Like the musicians, the dancers **improvised**, using varied and animated movements, including pushing, pulling and spinning.

Amazing Fact

Swing Kids

During the late 1930s, Europe was heading towards war. In Germany a group of teenagers known as the Swing Kids gathered together whenever possible, dancing swing and generally trying to follow the British and American way of life. This behaviour went against the beliefs of the Hitler Youth, the Nazis' organization for children and young adults. On 18 August 1941, over 300 Swing Kids were arrested. Punishments ranged from cutting their hair and sending them back to school under close watch, to being imprisoned in **concentration camps**.

▲ The Lindy hop was young, energetic and exciting, performed to the new jazz music that was being played in dance halls during the 1930s and 40s.

Famous Dances

Paso doble

The paso doble, meaning two-step, is based on music played at Spanish bull fights. It is different from other Latin dances as it originated in Spain, rather than Africa or South America, then swept across Europe in the 1930s. It is a stylized representation of the bullfight, with the man playing the part of the **matador** (bull fighter) and the woman playing the part of the matador's cape, the bull or even, sometimes, a **flamenco** dancer.

In the paso doble, the man imitates a matador. The woman takes on the role of his flowing red cape, or of a sultry flamenco dancer.

Dance as distraction

Dance halls throughout Europe helped to raise spirits during World War II. Every town and village had a hall where dancing could take place, so people could meet and forget the horrors of the war. Large dance halls had orchestras and smaller ones had small bands or played records. As in World War I, difficult dances were abandoned for easier ones, such as the waltz, foxtrot, quickstep and samba.

Latin links

Between 1942 and 1945, more than one and a half million US servicemen moved to Britain. Among other things, they brought with them the jive. It caught on immediately although, like new dances before, it seemed outrageous to some. A fast dance, where partners hold opposite hands, it is similar to swing and the lindy hop and it requires a lot of space. It probably developed from African slave dances in America, although some say it is based on Seminole Native American dances. It first became popular across the United States in the 1920s. The jive is a variation of the jitterbug and is included as one of the five International Latin dances (see pages 42–3).

Mambo developed in Cuba from the American influence on the rumba. American GIs danced swing moves to rumba music that was sped up, and the Cubans said they 'danced like mambos' (a mambo is a **voodoo** priestess). The rumba is a slow dance with the theme of courtship between a man and a woman. It started as an African ritual dance and became noticed in Cuba in the 1890s. 'Samba' means to pray, and the dance began as a way of calling gods and inducing trances in worshippers. It is a mixture of African steps and Brazilian rhythms that also emerged in the United States and Europe at the beginning of the 20th century.

Biography

Carmen Miranda

The singer and dancer Carmen Miranda (1909–55) is largely responsible for the surge in popularity of the samba in the 1940s. Nicknamed 'the Brazilian Bombshell', at one point she was one of the most successful film stars in the world. She wore exotic costumes (decorated with lots of plastic fruit!) and her singing and dancing were energetic and sensuous.

▶ Vivacious and attractive, Carmen Miranda popularized the samba in the 1940s and 50s.

Creative choreography

The word '**choreography**' came into common use in the 1950s. It means the art of creating dances and comes from the Greek *choros*, meaning dance, and *graphia*, meaning to write down. Although early dance teachers used to write down steps, **tempos** and patterns, over the last century ballroom and Latin dances have developed more through fashions than written instructions. TV programmes about dancing from around 40 years ago look dated today, yet the dances themselves are basically the same. It is all to do with trends and how certain steps and actions become attractive at certain times.

Social customs and strict rules

When social dancing began, choreography happened as people watched, followed others and handed down dances through generations. In the 16th century, dance teachers travelled around, teaching both city (upright and formal) and country (bouncy and fun) versions of dances, until both styles fused together.

These days, there are set guidelines for dances. They have to be performed to particular **rhythms** and with certain **stances** – especially in competitions. A few dances (such as the cha-cha-cha and waltz) have precise movements and timing, but most are open to some **improvization.** The ways in which partners hold or respond to each other is often set in these guidelines, and choreographers must take these factors into account when designing dances.

Choreographers must ensure that dancers use the entire floor – sometimes having to snake between other dancers – whilst still maintaining tempo and performing the correct steps and **figures.** A good choreographer will include some exciting or unexpected moves in their dances and will make sure that the dancers are able to incorporate these moves seamlessly. They may also 'borrow' steps from some dances and incorporate them into others. Many dances, such as the paso doble (see page 22) tell a story, and it is up to the choreographer to make sure that the story is told clearly.

▲ Dance teachers make up steps for their students, making sure that they adhere to the rules, go with the music and take up the entire floor.

Dance Facts

Early choreographer
In the 15th century, dance teachers such as Domenico da Piacenza (see page 8) began writing down steps. He composed dances for some of the most influential Italian families of the time, and also danced with them at important occasions. He opened a dance school and his manual on dance, published in about 1416, is the oldest to survive into modern times.

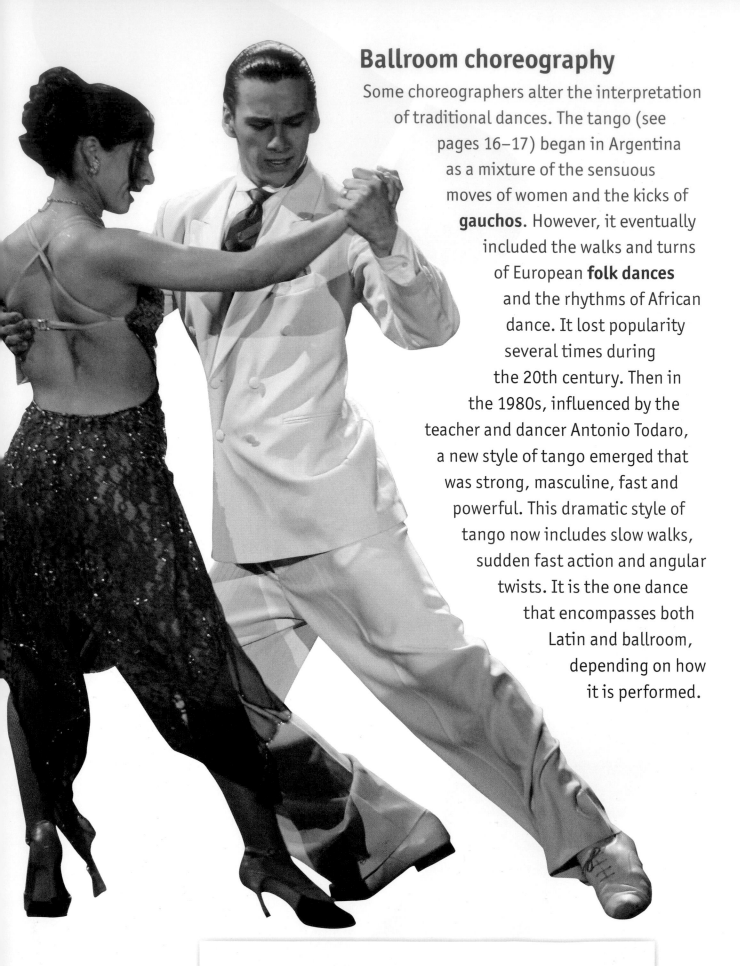

Ballroom choreography

Some choreographers alter the interpretation of traditional dances. The tango (see pages 16–17) began in Argentina as a mixture of the sensuous moves of women and the kicks of **gauchos**. However, it eventually included the walks and turns of European **folk dances** and the rhythms of African dance. It lost popularity several times during the 20th century. Then in the 1980s, influenced by the teacher and dancer Antonio Todaro, a new style of tango emerged that was strong, masculine, fast and powerful. This dramatic style of tango now includes slow walks, sudden fast action and angular twists. It is the one dance that encompasses both Latin and ballroom, depending on how it is performed.

▲ The 21st-century tango has moved on from its mixed origins. Now choreographers aim to create a balance of passion and aggression.

Ballroom essentials

All choreographers must know the essentials of all the main dances. For ballroom, these dances are the waltz, foxtrot, tango, Viennese waltz and quickstep.

- *Waltz* – The music has three beats to the bar. The steps are even and the man leads the woman. Using the **closed hold** throughout and keeping an erect **posture**, the couple rise, fall and turn.
- *Foxtrot* – Dancers use the closed hold and mirror each other's movements. The man steps outside the woman in the feather step. The woman turns on her heels, so the man must keep perfect balance for both of them.
- *Tango* – The knees are slightly flexed and leg control is necessary to produce the **staccato**, stalking style. The feet drag, stab and kick, while the arms and spine remain firm.
- *Viennese waltz* – The feet must be precise and posture remains straight, even when couples 'contra check' – that is, stop then reverse direction. They also turn whilst travelling across the floor.
- *Quickstep* – This is characterized by quick, light **pivots**. The basic lockstep, where one foot crosses behind the other, allows partners to turn and twist around the floor. Quickstep must include smooth, gliding action and fast kicks and flicks.

▼ Fred Astaire did his own choreography (often with Hermes Pan). He would rehearse for months with his partners to achieve that effortless effect.

Biography

Fred Astaire
Fred Astaire (1899–1987) was an American film and Broadway stage dancer, choreographer, singer and actor. He choreographed all his own routines, usually with another choreographer. He made over 30 musicals, 10 with his most famous partner, Ginger Rogers. Often acknowledged as the most influential dancer in the history of musicals, Astaire's technical control and sense of rhythm were amazing. He was elegant, graceful and original, and he expressed the romance of ballroom dancing perfectly.

Latin choreography

Since they developed in the 20th century, Latin and ballroom dancing have been linked together, because so many dances take steps from the same roots. Latin dances, like ballroom, have developed through society and fashion. The main Latin dances are cha-cha-cha, samba, rumba, paso doble and jive.

- *Cha-cha-cha* – Often just called the cha-cha, this dance is precise but also loose and strong. Leg lines are often parallel, toes are turned out and the weight shifts from one foot to the other. Similar to the rumba, it has to look spontaneous.

▼ Leg lines are often parallel in the cha-cha.

Biography

Victor Silvester

Victor Silvester (1900–1978) was a British dancer, composer and dance band leader. He played a major part in the development of ballroom dancing during the early 20th century. In 1922 he won the first World Standard Ballroom Dancing Championship and was a founder member of the Ballroom Committee of the Imperial Society of Teachers of Dancing. He published the first book about the new standards in 1928 and opened a chain of dance studios where he taught some top celebrities. In 1935 he formed his own five-piece band. By 1958, when he published his autobiography, he was the most successful dance band leader in British musical history and a major star on British radio and television.

▲ Dancing like this requires expert choreography and a lot of practice.

- *Samba* – Fast, fluid and strong, the samba demands precision and loose hips. The focus is on straight legs, following complex drum rhythms. It includes voltas and crossing of the feet – either in a circle or on the spot – and the hold is open and relaxed.

- *Rumba* – The rumba is based around the classic Latin-American hold, which is similar to the closed hold, only the partners are even closer! The couple also move apart and together during the dance. In the rope spin, the man supports the woman with his right arm while she spins on the balls of her feet and whips round. It has to look as if the dancers are floating on air, but it can become vigorous at times.

- *Paso doble* – A high degree of flexibility is necessary in the paso doble. Both partners have to bend and stretch, with a dramatic, proud posture, while their feet tell the story (they are to attract the bull's attention). **Flamenco** moves are often included in this dance.

- *Jive* – Fancy footwork characterizes the jive. Feet turn outwards, with kicks from the hip and flicks from the knee. This is far less rigid than other Latin dances – the body posture must adapt to any of the athletic moves in the routine.

Moving to the music

Each Latin and ballroom dance has to be performed to music with certain **rhythms** and beats. Music has always inspired and led the style of the dance, and dances only become popular if the music is appealing. Often, dances become known by the same name as the music – such as the waltz and **ragtime**.

▼ The orchestra plays a waltz to accompany the dancers.

Dance Facts

Waltz music

The waltz was named after the old German word *walzen*, meaning to roll, turn or glide. The music is in 3/4 time with a strong accent on the first beat. In the 17th century, waltzes were played in Vienna and in 1754 the first music for the 'Waltzen' appeared in Germany. One of the biggest boosts to the waltz came in around 1830, when two Austrian composers – Franz Lanner and Johann Strauss – wrote and played popular waltzes. These two composers set the standard for the Viennese waltz, which is danced at a **tempo** of about 180 beats per minute. Waltzes continue to be composed by modern composers.

Music sources

Dance music evolves from a variety of sources, just as the dances do. For instance, mambo began in Cuba in the 1940s. The name described both music and a dance style that took rhythms from Africa and North America. The mixture of swing and Cuban music produced a fascinating rhythm and a new entrancing dance to go with it.

During the 1940s, as everyone tried to dance the fast mambo, orchestras began slowing the music down and a new dance was introduced to go with the easier pace. The scraping and shuffling of the feet in these steps produced a sound like 'cha-cha-cha'. The cha-cha, as it is now called, can be danced to many styles of music including Latin, rock and roll, hip-hop and country and western.

Technique

Syncopation

Syncopation is a major characteristic of Latin music. It is an aspect of rhythm where the stress or emphasis shifts from the main, strong beat to the weak or quiet beats in a bar. Latin dance highlights these shifts by putting different emphasis on different steps, following the rhythm of the music.

▲ Dancing to live music remains popular – it is also how new dances develop. Someone creates a new move and others either add to it or follow. These salsa musicians and dancers are performing in Cuba.

Mambo also forms the basis of salsa, which developed during the late 20th century. Mambo is written in 4/4 time (four beats to a bar of music). Salsa is Spanish for 'hot sauce' and evolved from a blend of Afro-Cuban and Puerto Rican music with rock and jazz. Its roots are in the Latin dance music of the 1940s, which used trumpets and flutes, and it continues to influence music today.

Live music

At the start of the 20th century, ragtime and big bands were particularly popular in dance halls. People have always loved dancing to live music and, as big bands played the new swing style, people invented new dances to go with it. These included the jive, which became one of the approved ballroom dances.

Influences on Latin music

Latin music was influenced by Latin American people, including Haitians, Puerto Ricans, the Spanish and the Portuguese. It also absorbed influences from English and American music and, particularly, African music. The samba, rumba and cha-cha originated in Latin America, whereas the paso doble originated in Europe and the jive developed in North America. The paso doble is often **choreographed** to a piece of music known as the 'Spanish Gypsy Dance'. It is the same music that is regularly used at the beginning of a bullfight.

Biography

Cugat and Prado

Xavier Cugat (1900–90) was a Spanish-Cuban bandleader who helped to make Latin music popular in the early 20th century. Cugat moved to Cuba from Spain as a child and trained as a classical violinist, later moving to New York. He made records for the tango, conga, mambo, cha-cha and twist.

Pérez Prado (1916–89) was a Cuban-Mexican bandleader and composer, commonly called the 'King of the Mambo'. In 1948 he moved to Mexico, formed his own band and helped to popularize Latin music outside the Latino communities.

Getting into the mood

The process of turning pop songs into live dance music is not straightforward. The first thing to consider when choosing music is the beat. The beat has to suit the particular dance exactly. The second thing is the mood. For instance, doing the paso doble to pop music is possible, but the music must be dramatic to reflect the story, or the dance will fail. The choice of music can bring a new dimension to a dance. For instance, a samba can be performed to almost any lively music as long as it has 50 bars per minute. The cha-cha should be 30-32 bars per minute, and the rumba must be 27 bars per minute.

Costumes and make-up

Costumes and make-up

Like the dances, dance clothes are more complicated than they look! They have to look good, help to tell a story and not tear, slip or undo while the dancer is moving. As dance becomes more of an athletic sport, dance costume designers have to be highly skilled. Although it has not always been such a specialized business, dancing costumes have been important for centuries. Many dances have even had an influence on fashions of the day.

◀ As high society discovered a love of dancing, clothes were designed to look spectacular swirling about the ballrooms. This painting called *The Ball* by James Tissot was done in about 1878.

Fashion forward

Since the 19th century, fashions have been affected by popular dancing styles. From about 1811, women's dance dresses rose above the ankles and men wore fitted trousers, so that dances of the day could be danced more easily. Towards the end of the century, the waltz slowed down and ladies' fashions changed from full crinolines to more fitted dresses, allowing for closer contact between partners.

Even the fabrics were chosen to suit the dancing. Silks were acceptable for married women, who only danced a bit at balls, while unmarried women who danced a lot wore clothes made of light materials, such as muslin, cotton and lace. Most gentlemen wore a simple black dress coat, black breeches or trousers and a white shirt. Both ladies and gentlemen wore gloves to dance in, and they carried a spare pair in case the first became soiled.

Dance shoes

Dance shoes at the turn of the 20th century were made from silk, fabric or kid leather with straps and buttons. By the 1920s the charleston was all the rage, but so was the excitement about the discovery in Egypt of the tomb of the ancient pharaoh, Tutankhamun. Fashionable shoes were designed to reflect the craze for everything Egyptian, and to be suitable for dancing the charleston.

Dance Facts

Trendsetter

In the early 20th century, American couple Irene and Vernon Castle helped spread the new dance crazes (such as **ragtime** and the tango; see page 15). Irene became a major fashion trendsetter, bobbing her hair and wearing shorter skirts, without a corset! She danced in the **couture** clothes of designer Lucile and she also designed some of her clothes herself. When she wore white satin shoes for dancing, people followed her lead and the stores sold out of them.

▲ Latin dance clothes, like this samba costume, have always been more exotic and revealed more flesh than those for ballroom dancing.

Male fashions today

These days, men wear special dance trousers made of a stretch fabric, with long legs so that no leg or sock shows as they move. The trousers have high waists so that shirts stay tucked in, and they have extra fabric between the legs to allow them to move freely. Even so, male dancers always wear black underpants – just in case their trousers split mid-dance! Jackets are tailored so that even when arms are lifted, the shoulders remain flat and smooth without riding up. Sleeves are extra long so that they do not ride up, and shirts are either longer than usual or they fasten between the legs.

Stage and screen

Dance costumes have to be designed well in advance, as making them is time-consuming and expensive. Dance competitions, films and shows such as *Strictly Come Dancing*, *Dancing with the Stars*, *Dancing on Ice* and *Strictly Ballroom*, have meant that dance costumes have become practically works of art. Designers, suppliers, stylists and make-up artists work for hours behind the scenes to create costumes for the shows and films. For TV shows, for instance, the costumes are designed six months in advance.

Designers have more freedom when creating costumes for television or film rather than for competitions, as there are fewer rules. Generally a team of people works on each garment. The team usually consists of one designer, one or two machinists and someone who applies embellishments. Costumes are designed to enhance and flatter each dancer, and to fit in with the theme of the dance. Fabrics can be expensive and intricate trimmings are applied by hand. Costumes worn for Latin dances always show more flesh and are often in stronger or darker colours than ballroom costumes.

▼ Ballroom dance costumes can be frothy and light, to emphasize the style of the dance.

Competition dancewear has a stricter 'code' than stage or screen dancewear. For ballroom, men wear ties and a tailcoat or **tuxedo**, sometimes with a **cummerbund**, and women wear long or mid-calf length ball gowns. For Latin, men wear shirts, and women wear shorter, stretchy dresses, often with **asymmetrical** hemlines and plenty of rhinestones (imitation gemstones) or fringes!

Hair and make-up

Costumes enhance performances in a variety of ways. They help the dancers to feel the part, to 'tell the story' and they can create a spectacular vision. The impact of each costume is reinforced by music, lighting and hair and make-up.

Hair and make-up may be the last thing considered when it comes to dancing, but often they are the first thing to be noticed, and they can let the entire costume down if they aren't right. They must suit the style of the dance, and work with every other element of the performance, complementing the music, the **choreography** and the costume. Ballroom styles of hair and make-up tend to be soft and elegant, while those of Latin dancing are slicker and more dramatic.

▼ In shows and competitions, a little make up enhances the effect of the costume and helps dancers to feel the part.

Different dances, different outfits

Fashion has also always played a role in dance clothes. In the early 20th century, dancers often wore designers' couture clothes. These days, dance costumes need to stretch and to be fitted more closely to dancers' bodies. For ballroom dances, costumes tend to be flowing and made in fabrics that drape and ripple, often just skimming the floor. The clothes are light enough to move with the dancer's body, accentuating the **rhythm** of the dance. For Latin dances, clothes tend to be revealing, slinky and sparkling, to draw attention to the litheness of movement and origins of the dances.

In the West, as dancing is becoming more acrobatic, dancewear is shrinking! In a way, this provides greater challenges for designers as they have to make sure that only some parts of the body are exposed and other parts remain covered. Each dance has its own style, and the dancewear should reflect this.

Dance Facts

Dance cards

In the early 19th century, dance cards were how ladies kept track of the gentlemen they had promised to dance with. A small pencil was attached by a cord to the card, which was suspended from the lady's belt. The front cover told of the occasion, the location, time and date. Inside the card was a list of the evening's dances, with spaces for the gentlemen's names.

Learning Latin and ballroom

Most Latin and ballroom dancers begin dancing from an early age, and usually also learn ballet, tap and jazz. Of those three, ballet is probably the most important form of dance, as it teaches poise, **deportment** and flexibility, and helps the dancer create long, graceful 'lines' with their body. Dancing and teaching dancing require years of training, dedication and discipline. No matter how famous or accomplished a dancer becomes, they must always attend daily classes or practice sessions, to keep their bodies in peak condition and to maintain control over their muscles and movements.

Stamina and strength

To make difficult dances look effortless, dancers must build up their stamina and strength. Male dancers must be strong enough to lift their partners, yet they cannot have bulky muscles that will spoil the elegant lines when they're dancing, or restrict any of their movements. So most male dancers do special exercises to gain strength and control along with their normal training. Prior to a performance, all dancers warm up, gradually building up to fairly strenuous exercises that involve the feet, ankles and knees.

▶ Even the shortest dance requires lengthy rehearsals.

Dancing careers

Dancers mainly choose to become either performers or teachers, and many performers also teach to supplement their income or when they no longer dance full time. As well as teaching, dancers can also become **choreographers**, **artistic directors** or **dance physiotherapists**. The majority of performers dance in competitions, in film or on television, on cruise ships or in stage shows.

Certain qualifications are necessary to teach dance, and many dance teachers study for degrees at university for three or four years. They follow this with a teaching diploma. Others simply gain recognition and prizes for their dancing, then obtain a diploma to teach what they do best. Teachers should hold a teaching qualification from a recognized association, such as the International Dance Teachers' Association.

▶ International professional dancers like this couple must keep in peak condition. They dance every day, keep up with the latest dance styles and steps – and go for auditions for dancing parts.

Biography

Lilia Kopylova

Lilia Kopylova began ice skating and ballet when she was 4 years old. She won the Moscow championship in figure skating at the age of 6. She began ballroom dancing when she was 9, and was a ballroom and Latin champion by the age of 15. She moved to England in 1997 and has been hugely successful in competitions, both alone and with her husband, Darren Bennett. She has danced in TV shows since 2004.

Competitions

As dance becomes more athletic, theatrical producers require professional dancers to be ever more highly trained and to be able to perform all forms of dance to a high standard. Most performers have to overcome stiff competition, and they train strenuously for hours each day to achieve high enough standards. This has a knock-on effect on **amateur** dancers who enter competitions, as their standards are becoming higher too.

International Standard and International Latin

Since the mid-20th century, the range of competitive dances has expanded, although the classification of ballroom dances has always been fluid, with new dances being added or removed occasionally. Five Latin dances (cha-cha, samba, rumba, paso doble and jive) joined the five 'standard' ballroom dances of waltz, tango, foxtrot, quickstep and Viennese waltz. They are now known as International Standard and International Latin. Sometimes these competitions are also called 'ten-dance', as they consist of ten dances.

Contestants conform to rigid discipline, which requires hours of practice and financial commitment. These means that modern ballroom dancing is much closer to being a professional sport than social dancing ever was. In 1997, the International DanceSport Federation (IDSF) became recognized by the International Olympic Committee as being responsible for DanceSport throughout the world. 'DanceSport' then replaced the word 'ballroom' in the description of this competitive dancing, reflecting the sporting values of this physically demanding activity. DanceSport now includes all the International Standard dances, along with a sports-based culture.

American Style dances (American Smooth and American Rhythm) are less precise and competitive forms of social dancing. In American Style, divisions between styles and rules about steps and clothes are less strict than in DanceSport.

▲ Dancing couples compete for the highest awards and recognition in international dance competitions. There are four million registered competitors for DanceSport, from 85 countries.

Technique

Competition divisions

Competitive dancers are usually amateurs. In some US dance competitions, couples that combine one professional and one amateur are allowed to compete. In professional dancing, age does not matter – dancers are judged on their ability alone. In amateur competitive dancing, however, performers are placed into groups: Juveniles (up to 12), Juniors (up to 16), Youth (up to 21), Adult Amateurs (age 16+), Seniors (age 35+) or over-45s (age 45+). Then, within the age groups, couples are divided by experience levels into the following classes: Beginners, Novice, Intermediate, Pre-Championships (which is also called Pre-Amateur) and Open Amateur.

Costume design

Many dance costume designers began as dancers themselves, while others were trained in art or fashion design, or in costume design. Dance costume designers might work alone or as part of a large team. If working in a team, such as in a TV production company or on film set, they might have to oversee costume design assistants, wardrobe supervisors, dressers, commercial hire companies, specialist craftspeople, milliners (hat-makers) and jewellers. Most dance costume designers are extremely creative. They also have a good understanding of dance moves and the requirements of the dancers.

Set design

These days, set design for ballroom and Latin dancing often requires more than just a smooth floor and some lights! Just as music, choreography and costumes can enhance the mood of a dance, so visual elements such as props, lighting and stage sets may also amplify certain qualities of the dance movement. Apart from having special floors (see box), the best sets, whether they are ballrooms or TV studios, are those where the audience has a full, panoramic (all-round) view of the dancers. The lighting must not cast ugly shadows or obscure the dancers' movements. It can be used to add colour and shape to the dance. For TV programmes such as *Strictly Come Dancing* or *Dancing with the Stars*, studios are usually set up a couple of days in advance, and dismantled directly after each show. This is because the studios are used for other programmes during the week, so set designers need to be flexible and imaginative!

Amazing Fact

Floor quality
The most important part of a dance competition or show's set is the floor. It must be bouncy enough to give the dancers' legs good shock absorption, but if it is for television or film, it must also be light enough to be taken apart. For this reason, most of these temporary floors are made of a combination of metal, concrete, cladding and plywood.

Dancing films

Films, TV programmes and shows have stimulated many people's passion for dancing. From Fred and Ginger in the 1930s and 1940s, to *Dirty Dancing* in 1987, *Strictly Ballroom* in 1992 and *Tango* in 1998, the techniques of the performers, along with their costumes and sets, often inspire new approaches and crazes around the world.

▼ Costumes, steps and sets have evolved over the years, keeping Latin and ballroom dancing fashionable and contemporary.

Glossary

amateur someone who dances as a non-professional – that is, they are not paid to dance

aristocrat member of the upper class or nobility

artistic director person who is responsible for the creative content of a dance

asymmetrical not balanced, usually different on either side

choreography art of creating dances

closed hold when the man's left hand holds his partner's right hand high. The woman's left hand rests on the top of the man's right upper arm, and his right hand rests on her back.

concentration camps places where people were imprisoned under harsh conditions

couture high fashion

cummerbund broad sash worn around a man's waist

dance physiotherapist someone who treats and prevents dancers' injuries

deportment the way a person stands and holds themselves

figures standard movements that dancers perform in different dances

flamenco Spanish gypsy dance, usually accompanied by Spanish guitar

folk dance traditional dance, nearly always for groups of people to do together for a particular occasion, often to mark something that happens every year

gaucho Argentinian cowboy

improvisation making something up on the spot, in dance or music

matador Spanish bull fighter

pivot rotate or turn

posture attitude or pose

processional dance dance where couples follow each other around the room in a parade

professional someone who earns money from dancing

ragtime music that emerged in the 1890s in African-American communities. It was a mix of European folk (traditional) music and African drum rhythms.

regulate control by the use of rules and restrictions

rhythm timing system, based on sound

staccato in a short and abrupt manner

stances ways of positioning the body

tempo speed in music

tuxedo man's dress jacket with satin lapels

voodoo religion based on mystical beliefs and the power of nature, that originated in Africa

Further information

Books

Jennifer Blizin Gillis, *Ballroom Dancing for Fun*, Compass Point Books (2007)

Andrée Grau, *Dance*, Dorling Kindersley (2005)

Harriet R. Lihs, *Appreciating Dance*, Princeton Book Company (2002)

Victor Silvester, *Modern Ballroom Dancing*, Ebury Press (2005)

Websites

www.ballroomdancers.com

A website offering information on all kinds of ballroom dancing, from swing to Latin, smooth to hustle.

www.dancing-times.co.uk

The website of Britain's leading dance monthly magazine. Includes information on all kinds of topical dance.

www.bbc.co.uk/strictlycomedancing

The official website of the BBC programme *Strictly Come Dancing*, including information on past series and dance classes across Britain.

http://abc.go.com/primetime/dancingwiththestars/index?pn=about

The official website of the ABC programme, including information about dancers, dances and music.

www.dancesport.uk.com/world.htm

World dance associations and links to major ballroom dance websites in the world.

Index